Answers to Your Questions about Heaven

Answers to your
questions about
HEAVEN

David Jeremiah

Tyndale House Publishers, Inc.
Carol Stream, Illinois

Visit Tyndale online at www.tyndale.com.

TYNDALE and Tyndale's quill logo are registered trademarks of Tyndale House Publishers, Inc.

Answers to Your Questions about Heaven

Previously published in 2013 as *Answers to Questions about Heaven* by Turning Point. First printing by Tyndale House Publishers, Inc., in 2015.

Designed by Nicole Grimes

Published in association with Yates & Yates (www.yates2.com).

Library of Congress Cataloging-in-Publication Data

Jeremiah, David.
  [Answers to Questions about Heaven]
  Answers to your questions about heaven / David Jeremiah.
    pages cm
  "Previously published in 2013 as Answers to Questions about Heaven by Turning Point."
  Includes bibliographical references.
  ISBN 978-1-4964-0212-7 (hc)
1. Heaven—Christianity—Miscellanea. I. Title.
  BT846.3.J465 2015
  236'.24—dc23   2014028035

Printed in the United States of America

21	20	19	18	17	16	15
7	6	5	4	3	2	1

Contents

Introduction

What comes to mind when you think of heaven? Clouds and harps? Spires and domes? Most people form their impressions of heaven from television, movies, and their imaginations rather than a careful study of Scripture. But the Bible contains over five hundred references to heaven. It provides a virtual travelogue for God's children, with detailed information about our eternal home. After spending years studying this subject in Scripture, I'm overwhelmed by the comprehensive information God has given. He offers specific answers to our natural questions. In this book I've tried to share these answers as simply, readably, and biblically as possible.

After all, it's strengthening to turn our minds toward home and toward Him. The Bible says, "If then you were raised with Christ, seek those things which are above, where Christ is, sitting at the right hand of God. Set your mind on things above, not on things on the earth" (Colossians 3:1-2).

During the Second World War, when it was hard for Franklin Roosevelt to travel among the troops because of his disability, First Lady Eleanor Roosevelt took his place, and she became a favorite of soldiers around the world. She sent cables and letters back to FDR, becoming his eyes and ears. On one such trip in the Pacific theater she spent an evening talking to a group of soldiers, and later told her husband there was only one thought on all their minds—the desire to finish the battle so they could go home.[1]

That's how God's children feel about heaven. We're deployed on planet Earth, but it's only a temporary assignment. Goodness and mercy will surely follow us all the days of our lives. But what we're really anticipating is dwelling in the house of the Lord forever.

That's what this book is all about!

David Jeremiah
SPRING 2015

What's Up with Heaven?

WHY SHOULD I STUDY HEAVEN WHILE I'M LIVING ON EARTH?

∽◦∾

Did you know that heaven is mentioned more than five hundred times in the Scriptures? Being a prominent teaching in the Bible, heaven ought to also be prominent in our hearts and in our thoughts. As we become more heavenly minded, we actually become of more earthly good!

God has placed within our hearts a hunger for eternity, a hunger for heaven. And if we do not understand that and we do not feed that hunger with the spiritual truth of the Word of God, we will end up trying to satisfy that hunger with vain and tawdry things that will leave us empty and without satisfaction.

The truth is, we can never approximate all that God has prepared for us in our heavenly home. And we cannot recreate heaven on earth. But when we choose to focus on and prepare for the eternal home that awaits us, our earthly focus is shifted toward living a life that honors God and leads others to Him.

> *We can never approximate all that God has prepared for us in our heavenly home.*

IS HEAVEN A REAL, PHYSICAL PLACE?

Heaven is no figment of the imagination; nor is it a feeling, a state of mind, or the invention of man.

> *Heaven is a literal place prepared by Christ for a prepared people.*

Heaven is a literal place prepared by Christ for a prepared people. In John chapter 14, Jesus Himself leaves His disciples with this promise:

> In My Father's house are many mansions; if it were not so, I would have told you. I go to prepare a place for you. And if I go and prepare a place for you, I will come again and receive you to Myself; that where I am, there you may be also.
>
> JOHN 14:2-3

It is interesting to note that the Greek term translated *place* in this passage is actually the word *topos*, which more specifically refers to a locatable place.

From this promise we can have full confidence that heaven is a real, physical place—a place where believers will one day reside with their Savior!

HOW MANY LEVELS OF HEAVEN ARE DESCRIBED IN THE BIBLE?

The Bible speaks of three distinct heavens.

1. The first heaven is described in Isaiah 55:9-10 and is the atmosphere surrounding the earth— the domain of the clouds and birds (Genesis 1:20).

2. The second heaven is spoken of in Genesis 1:14-17 as the domain of the heavenly bodies: the sun, moon, stars, planets, and galaxies.

3. Paul described in his second letter to the Corinthians being "caught up to the third heaven" (2 Corinthians 12:2), which is beyond the first and second levels of heaven and is the dwelling place of God—where we will one day join Christ.

WHERE IS THE EXACT LOCATION OF HEAVEN?

~⊛~

We do not know precisely, but we know that it is "up." Ephesians 4:10 says that Christ "ascended far above all the heavens," meaning heaven is above us.

Even though we do not know the exact location, we know that heaven is a specific place being prepared for God's people.

However, "up" is a different locale depending on where you are located on the earth. Satan, addressing God in Isaiah 14:13, said, "I will ascend into heaven, I will exalt my throne above the stars of God; I will also sit on the mount of the congregation on the farthest sides of the north," which would indicate that heaven is located in the north. Even though we do not know the exact location, we know that it is a specific place being prepared for God's people.

—— ⁓ ——

Both the Old and New Testaments depict heaven as a place that is high, lofty, and lifted up. The Old Testament word for heaven is shamayim, *which means "the heights." And in the New Testament, the Greek word* ouranos *refers to heaven as that which is "raised up or lofty."*

—— ⁓ ——

IS IT POSSIBLE FOR A CHRISTIAN'S NAME TO BE "BLOTTED OUT" OF THE BOOK OF LIFE?

In order to understand how the Book of Life works, it may be necessary for us to better understand the Roman and Greek practices of the first century.

If a person dies having rejected God's offer of salvation, his name is blotted out of the Lamb's Book of Life.

Cities in John's day had a registry that contained the name of every person who lived within the confines of that city. But if a person defiled his citizenship, he could be called before the tribunal, and his name would be removed from the registry—literally "blotted out" of the city book as a penalty for his actions. He would no longer be considered a citizen of that particular metropolis, and he would be consigned either to live in anonymity or to move elsewhere.

With that concept in mind, I believe the Book of Life is a book originally containing the name of every person born into this world. But if a person dies having rejected God's offer of salvation, his name is blotted out of the Lamb's Book of Life.

WHAT IS THE LAMB'S BOOK OF LIFE, AND WILL MY NAME BE IN IT?

The Bible says that in heaven, there is a book, or a registry, called the Lamb's Book of Life. And the names of all who will be in heaven are recorded in that one book.

William R. Newell, a great Bible scholar, said there are four things to be noted about the Book of Life:

1. It is the absence of one's name, not one's good works, that dooms a person.
2. Evil works are not the issue. Many of earth's greatest sinners' names are recorded in the Book of Life because they accepted God's offer of salvation.
3. Those whose names do not appear in the Book are cast into the lake of fire (Revelation 20:15).
4. All names found in the Book were written before the Judgment Day. There is no record of names being recorded (decisions being made) on that day.[2]

Revelation 21:27 says "there shall by no means enter [into heaven] anything that defiles, or causes an abomination or a lie, but only those who are written in the Lamb's Book of Life."

Christ is the only way to heaven. And one day, Jesus will say to those who rejected Him, "I never knew you; depart from Me" (Matthew 7:23).

We cannot earn our passage to heaven simply by being "good" people or by living "good" lives. Ultimately, we will not be granted entrance to heaven unless we repent of our sins and accept Jesus as our Lord and Savior—then we can have full confidence that our names are recorded in the Book of Life.

> *I am the way, the truth, and the life. No one comes to the Father except through Me.*
>
> —John 14:6

Where Are They Now?

DO OUR SOULS "SLEEP" UNTIL THE RESURRECTION AT THE RAPTURE?

When a believer dies, his body goes in the grave and goes to sleep. But his soul does not sleep; his soul and spirit go to Paradise.

In Scripture, "falling asleep" is a softened term for the believer's death. For instance, when Paul wrote to the Thessalonian believers, he said: "I do not want you to be ignorant, brethren, concerning those who have fallen asleep, lest you sorrow as others who have no hope" (1 Thessalonians 4:13). Paul wasn't talking about falling asleep the way we fall asleep at night. He was describing the death of Christians.

In the New Testament, the Greek word translated "to fall asleep" is *koimao*, which comes from the same Greek root as "to lie down." *Koimao* was also used to describe someone who slept in a hotel for one night and the next day would get up to continue his or her journey. This is a beautiful image of what happens to believers' bodies when they die. Their bodies go to sleep, awaiting the Resurrection at the Rapture—while their souls and spirits go to be with our Lord in heaven.

This is a beautiful image of what happens to believers' bodies when they die. Their bodies go to sleep, awaiting the Resurrection.

DOES A PERSON'S EARTHLY STATUS IN TERMS OF POSSESSIONS OR WEALTH AFFECT HIS OR HER ETERNAL RESTING PLACE?

13

While on earth, the rich man described in Luke 16:19-31 was clothed in purple and fine linen, had many servants, and ate sumptuous meals. In contrast, the poor man Lazarus was covered with sores, subsisted on crumbs, and had only dogs to care for him. What a contrast! And yet we learn that Lazarus went to Paradise, a place of comfort, while the rich man was sent to a place of misery. Only our spiritual status before God determines our eternal resting place.

Only our spiritual status before God determines our eternal resting place.

IS THERE AN INTERMEDIATE HEAVEN?

The Bible teaches that every believer who died prior to the ascension of Christ went to an intermediate heaven called Paradise, or Abraham's bosom (Luke 16:22, KJV).

But when Jesus ascended after His death, He went into Paradise and took all who were there—all the Old Testament saints, all who had died and believed in God before the Ascension—with Him to the third heaven (Ephesians 4:8-10).

This means that believers no longer go to the intermediate heaven upon death. The souls and spirits of today's believers go immediately to the third heaven because Paradise is no longer an intermediate place; Paradise is now with God (2 Corinthians 12:2-4).

IS THERE AN INTERMEDIATE HELL? WHAT ABOUT PURGATORY?

Yes—there is an intermediate hell. When an unbeliever dies, his body goes into the grave and his spirit and soul go to Hades.

Whatever decisions we make about eternity will be made in this life.

Revelation 20 tells us that "Death and Hades delivered up the dead" (verse 13). This passage indicates that Hades remains an intermediate hell until the Great White Throne Judgment— when "Death and Hades [will be] cast into the lake of fire" (verse 14)—the permanent hell.

But Hades is not a place of decision. There is no such place as purgatory. The Bible teaches that "it is appointed unto men once to die, but after this the judgment" (Hebrews 9:27, KJV).

In Luke 16:26, Abraham describes a "great gulf fixed" between Hades and Paradise, "so that those who want to pass from here to you cannot, nor can those from there pass to us." This passage illustrates the permanence of the gulf between heaven and hell. We won't be able to "cross" from one side to the other.

Whatever decisions we make about eternity will be made in this life.

---

*We then, as workers together with Him
also plead with you not to receive the
grace of God in vain. For He says:
"In an acceptable time I have heard you,
And in the day of salvation
I have helped you."*
—*2 Corinthians 6:1-2*

Angels and Death

WHAT ROLE DO ANGELS PLAY WHEN A BELIEVER DIES?

Did you know that when a person says, "The angels came and took him," it's not just sentiment? It's Scripture based! Jesus said that when the beggar Lazarus died, he "was carried by the angels to Abraham's bosom" (Luke 16:22). I believe Jesus included this detail to assure us that God sends His angels to usher believers into eternity.

So why do angels carry believers to heaven? The third heaven, where Jesus lives, is an incredible stretch of atmosphere from the earth. If the believer's spirit is to return to God, then it must pass through this great expanse. Angels take us to heaven so we won't have to make the journey alone. God sends His heavenly escorts to lead us home.

God sends His heavenly escorts to lead us home.

So it was that the beggar died, and was carried by the angels to Abraham's bosom. The rich man also died and was buried. And being in torments in Hades, he lifted up his eyes and saw Abraham afar off, and Lazarus in his bosom.
—Luke 16:22-23

What about the Children?

IN WHAT WAY DO WE HAVE TO BE LIKE CHILDREN TO GET INTO HEAVEN?

Jesus said, "I tell you the truth, unless you change and become like little children, you will never enter the kingdom of heaven. Therefore, whoever humbles himself like this child is the greatest in the kingdom of heaven" (Matthew 18:3-4, NIV). The Lord is telling us that the way we get to heaven is to humble ourselves as little children, to acknowledge that we can't earn our way to heaven by our good works, and to put our trust in Jesus Christ alone—plus or minus nothing. When we ask Him to forgive our sins and come into our hearts and to become the Lord of our lives, we make a reservation in heaven that is absolutely certain.

We can't earn our way to heaven by our good works.

IS THERE A SPECIFIC AGE OF ACCOUNTABILITY MENTIONED IN THE BIBLE?

There is no specific age mentioned in the Bible when a child would have an understanding of the message of the gospel. Until children mature and gain an understanding of what the message of Christ's sacrifice on the cross means to them person-

Until children mature and gain an understanding of what the message of Christ's sacrifice on the cross means to them personally and realize their sin and guilt before God, they are covered by the blood of Christ.

ally and realize their sin and guilt before God, they are covered by the blood of Christ (Matthew 19:14; James 4:17). This principle also applies to those who, while they are mature physically, have never matured mentally or emotionally. They may be in mature bodies, but their minds are childlike.

WHAT ABOUT CHILDREN LOST THROUGH MISCARRIAGES OR ABORTIONS?

Concerning the unborn, we have it on the authority of Scripture that a child is a person from the moment of conception (Psalm 139:13). Based on that truth, all these unborn ones, for whatever reason they have been unborn, will be taken directly to heaven by the Father. And, one day, if we have believed in Christ, we will see our lost little ones again. Remember, our Savior has compassion for little children and infants, and He is not willing that even one of them should perish.

> *Our Savior has compassion for little children and infants, and He is not willing that even one of them should perish.*

HOW OLD WILL CHILDREN BE IN HEAVEN?

⸙

While there is no absolute answer provided in Scripture concerning this question, there are different views to consider.

> *The book of Revelation describes worship in heaven as an all-encompassing act involving everyone who is there.*

Some suggest that when we arrive in heaven, we will all be mature in body and mind and spirit. The book of Revelation describes worship in heaven as an all-encompassing act involving everyone who is there. Therefore, whoever is in heaven will be of such an age so as to be able to participate in the eternal worship of almighty God.

Others hold that if the Millennium is part of heaven, there's reason to believe that children will be in heaven and allowed to grow up until they reach a mature age.

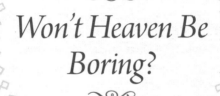

Won't Heaven Be Boring?

WILL THERE BE WORK TO DO IN HEAVEN? OR WILL WE SIT IDLY?

～◌～

Be assured that we are not going to sit idly in heaven.

What is God going to say to us when we get to heaven? I don't think He will say, "Well done, good and faithful servant; you can have the rest of eternity off." He will say, "Well done, good and faithful servant; you were faithful over a few things, I will make you ruler over many things. Enter into the joy of your lord" (Matthew 25:21). Now, that doesn't sound like we're going to be sitting around forever and ever—it sounds like there will be "many things" to do! For one, we already know that we'll be ruling and reigning with Christ over this renovated earth during the Millennium.

And Revelation 22 says, "His servants shall serve Him" (verse 3). God has a great plan for each one of us to be wonderfully, happily, excitedly employed—serving the Lord in Paradise. And we will be serving in the fullest expression of the capacity God has given us and using the giftedness He has placed within us.

What we won't experience are the difficulties, pressures, stresses, and heartaches that accompany work down here. We cannot possibly comprehend all of the glorious work with which we'll be occupied throughout eternity; but we know that our service will result in deep joy and fulfillment.

---

*[In heaven] our minds and bodies will
never fade and we will never lack resources
or opportunity, [so] our work won't
degenerate. Buildings won't last for only
fifty years, and books won't be in print for
only twenty years. They'll last forever.*[3]
—Randy Alcorn

WILL HEAVEN EVER GROW BORING?

There is a fundamental reason that heaven will never be boring: God is not boring! God is the most exciting, adventuresome, creative Person that you can imagine—multiplied a thousand times over. We can't even comprehend a morsel of the excitement that is resident in the triune God with whom we are going to spend eternity.

The psalmist says that in His presence "is fullness of joy;" and at His "right hand are pleasures forevermore" (Psalm 16:11). When we get to heaven, when we are in the presence of God, everything we do will bring about perfect satisfaction and reward. We will never engage in anything that leaves us feeling even a tad bit empty. Everything we do will bring us absolute and total fulfillment and joy, because that's the way God has created us. In fact, Ecclesiastes 3 says that God has actually put eternity in our hearts. What this means is that God has built us with a space within us that can't be satisfied with anything except heaven. And that's the reason we aren't going to be bored in heaven—it's everything our hearts long for! In Paradise, we will finally feel the completeness that we were created to enjoy.

God has built us with a space within us that can't be satisfied with anything except heaven.

WHO ARE HEAVEN'S INHABITANTS?

In Hebrews 12:22-23 we find a list of some of heaven's residents: "You have come to Mount Zion and to the city of the living God, the heavenly Jerusalem, to an innumerable company of angels, to the general assembly and church of the firstborn who are registered in heaven, to God the Judge of all, to the spirits of just men made perfect." Believers are going to spend all of eternity with "an innumerable company of angels," all of the "just men made perfect" (the Old Testament saints), the people who are of the firstborn (the church). Above all, we're going to spend eternity with our God.

Believers are going to spend all of eternity with "an innumerable company of angels."

WILL WE HAVE FELLOWSHIP WITH ONE ANOTHER IN HEAVEN?

In heaven, we'll have fellowship like never before!

Because we will be God's people made over, we will be perfectly compatible with one another and able, for the first time ever, to enjoy the intimate fellowship that we all long for in our hearts.

And if heaven weren't exciting enough, imagine having the unlimited opportunity to fellowship with people from all ages of history—even people we've only read about in books.

There's a whole list of people I'd like to meet: David and Joseph and Daniel from the Old Testament, C. S. Lewis, Charles Haddon Spurgeon, Andrew Murray, A. W. Tozer, and many others.

What an incredible time of fellowship! We can't possibly comprehend it completely, but we're going to live together in community and be able to have unlimited fellowship with one another for all of eternity.

Imagine having the unlimited opportunity to fellowship with people from all ages of history—even people we've only read about in books.

WILL WE HAVE FELLOWSHIP WITH CHRIST IN HEAVEN?

In heaven, we won't just fellowship with the church and the angels. We will be able to know and fellowship with our Lord in a way that we cannot possibly comprehend. We are going to know Him—the same Lord Jesus who walked upon the streets of Galilee and healed the sick and ministered to those who were lame and blind, the same Lord Jesus with nail-scarred hands and the signs of redemption in His side. Our Savior will be our personal friend, and we will fellowship with Him forever and ever.

We are going to know Him—the same Lord Jesus who walked upon the streets of Galilee and healed the sick and ministered to those who were lame and blind, the same Lord Jesus with nail-scarred hands and the signs of redemption in His side.

What's Up with Angels?

WHY STUDY ANGELS?

There's a lot more to this "strange" subject of angels than we imagine. Mystery saturates this whole topic. But mystery is good and healthy for us, and maybe more now than ever. So many Christians today are lacking in awe and a sense of mystery when they consider the things of God. My prayer is that this presumption will start to be corrected as we gain respect for the secrets surrounding God's angels. Once we honestly investigate the amazing things Scripture tells us about them, we actually find ourselves drawn closer to God, instead of being distracted from God. And I believe that anyone who goes into a study of angels with a high view of God will come away with an even higher view of Him. All glory be to the God of the angels!

WHERE DO ANGELS RESIDE?

Heaven is the dwelling place of the angels because angels belong exclusively to God.

The best definition of heaven is that it's God's dwelling place. "Heaven is my throne," God says; and that is where angels work and live. They inhabit the throne room of God, because they belong to God. But also keep this in mind: when Paul tells us to set our minds on things above (Colossians 3:1-2), he points out specifically that heaven is where Christ is. Angels are there too, but Paul doesn't put them in the spotlight. It's Christ who can make us heavenly minded, not angels.

HOW MANY ANGELS ARE THERE IN EXISTENCE?

No precise count is given in Scripture, but there's plenty of evidence that they make up a mighty multitude. In Revelation 5:11, John says he saw "ten thousand times ten thousand, and thousands of thousands" of angels around the throne. To give you a perspective on how many angels this is, the average football stadium in America holds about 50,000 people. It would take some 2,000 stadiums of that size to hold 100,000,000 people. The total number of angels John saw may have far exceeded 100,000,000—10,000 was the highest numerical figure used in the Greek language. "Ten thousand times ten thousand" may have been John's way of describing an inexpressibly large company of angels. In fact, Hebrews 12:22 says, "You have come to Mount Zion and to the city of the living God, the heavenly Jerusalem, to an innumerable company of angels," indicating that the population of angels is so large that they cannot be numbered.

WHEN WERE ANGELS CREATED?

In the Old Testament the Lord told Job that angels were already on the scene to celebrate when the earth was created: "The LORD spoke to Job out of the storm. He

It's very likely the angels are older than anything in the world as we see it.

said: . . . 'Where were you when I laid the earth's foundation? Tell me, if you understand. . . . On what were its footings set, or who laid its cornerstone—while the morning stars sang together and all the angels shouted for joy?'" (Job 38:1, 4, 6-7, NIV). Job wasn't there when the earth was formed, but the angels were—and they were having a good time of it too (verse 7). So it's very likely the angels are older than anything in the world as we see it.

DO ANGELS EVER DIE?

In Daniel 9 the angel Gabriel appeared to the prophet Daniel. Then more than five hundred years later, this same unchanged Gabriel appeared to Zacharias, the father of John the Baptist (Luke 1:5-25). And in Luke 20:36 we read: "Nor can they die anymore, for they are equal to the angels and are sons of God, being sons of the resurrection."

As spiritual beings, angels know nothing of what it's like to become ill, grow old, and eventually die. Someday we, too, will be beyond the reach of those afflictions. We and the angels will share permanent citizenship in God's heavenly Kingdom forever.

HAS GOD CREATED MORE ANGELS SINCE THEIR INITIAL CREATION?

I have no biblical reason to believe that God has created any more angels. And apparently there's been no reduction in their number either, since angels do not die. Nor has there been any increase, since angels don't reproduce—according to Jesus' statement that angels don't marry: "In the resurrection they neither marry nor are given in marriage, but are like angels of God in heaven" (Matthew 22:30). We have as many angels today as we've ever had.

We have as many angels today as we've ever had.

DO ANGELS HAVE PHYSICAL BODIES LIKE HUMANS?

Angels are real but without material substance as we think of it. Hebrews 1:14 describes them as "ministering spirits sent forth to minister for those who will inherit salvation." They apparently have no physical nature, no breath or blood—God created them as nonphysical beings. If they occupy some form of permanent bodies, these would be spiritual bodies, perhaps like the ones we'll wear someday in eternity. It must be their spiritual nature—as well as their spiritual holiness—that allows angels the continual proximity to God they enjoy.

Angels are real but without material substance as we think of it.

ARE ANGELS OMNIPRESENT, OMNIPOTENT, OR OMNISCIENT LIKE GOD?

In their spiritual state, angels have many limitations that God can never have. For example, angels cannot be in more than one place at once, unlike God, who is everywhere at once. Only God is infinite in His whereabouts; He is omnipresent.

And as powerful as angels are, they are not omnipotent like God. They have no force of their own and are impotent without God. They can exercise only the power that God channels through them.

Angels are also limited in knowledge. Jesus said the angels don't know the time of His Second Coming to the world (Matthew 24:36). But God in heaven always knows the end from the beginning and can communicate His plans to whomever He chooses. Only He is omniscient, all-knowing, infinite in knowledge.

ARE DEPICTIONS OF ANGELS IN ART, LIKE CHILDLIKE CHERUBIM, ACCURATE?

We must not create or reshape angels according to our own fancy. Countless multitudes have fallen into this error. A majority of the angel representations we see—in paintings and gift books or as lapel pins and china figurines or gracing a host of other varieties of merchandise—are merely products of human imagination. So how exactly does the Bible describe angels? In Scripture, angels of God always appear in the masculine. Angels appearing as females show up in some historical accounts and in some personal experiences, but never in the Bible.

Daniel's account of the awesome figure he saw on the riverbank has been called Scripture's most detailed description of an angel's appearance:

> There before me was a man dressed in linen,
> with a belt of fine gold from Uphaz around
> his waist. His body was like topaz, his face like
> lightning, his eyes like flaming torches, his arms
> and legs like the gleam of burnished bronze,
> and his voice like the sound of a multitude. I,
> Daniel, was the only one who saw the vision;

those who were with me did not see it, but such terror overwhelmed them that they fled and hid themselves. So I was left alone, gazing at this great vision; I had no strength left, my face turned deathly pale and I was helpless.

DANIEL 10:5-8, NIV

In 2 Chronicles 32:21 we read that "the LORD sent an angel, who annihilated all the fighting men and the commanders and officers in the camp of the Assyrian king" (NIV). Divorced from any credibility forever are the thoughts of plump baby "cherubs" or pale ladies with transparent wings traced in glitter across Christmas cards. No, real angels have been and are and shall forever be awesome warriors for God.

ARE GOD'S ANGELS ALL THE SAME?

Each angel has his own job description and carries out God's will. To find out about the varied types and tasks of the angels, let's take a look at a few of the terms the Bible uses to reference angels.

Hosts: Throughout the Bible, angels are called "the hosts of the Lord." The word "host" comes from the Old Testament Hebrew word *tsaba* and the New Testament Greek word *stratia*. Both terms mean "a well-trained army"—one that is prepared for war. God's angels are organized and ready to respond to His every desire and command.

Seraphim: This term, which literally means "burning ones," is only mentioned in the book of Isaiah. These angels dwell so close to the presence of God that they burn with a holy brilliance. According to Isaiah chapter 6, the seraphim have six wings. Two wings cover their faces in reverence, two wings cover the seraphim's feet in humility, and two wings are for flying. The seraphim also have human features such as feet, hands, and voices.

Cherubim: Cherubim are angels that stand close to God's throne (and they don't even vaguely resemble the winged infants we usually think of as cherubs). The description in Ezekiel 10 suggests that cherubim have a more human appearance than the seraphim. Each cherub has four faces: the face of a man, the face of a lion, the face of an ox, and the face of an eagle. They have human hands and four wings instead of six. Unlike other angels, the cherubim never convey messages from God to people. They are also never directly called angels. The first time cherubim appear in the Bible is at the Garden of Eden (Genesis 3:24). God had the cherubim placed at the Garden with flaming swords to guard the tree of life after Adam and Eve were evicted from Paradise.

WHICH ANGELS ARE SPECIFICALLY NAMED IN THE BIBLE?

Scripture mentions two angels by name.

Michael: Michael is the only archangel mentioned by name in the Bible, and most scholars believe he is the only archangel—that he is the most prominent of all the angels. The term "archangel" occurs in the New Testament in the singular (Jude 1:9), whereas Daniel 10:13 refers to Michael as "one of the chief princes." It is generally believed that Michael's voice will be the one heard to announce the return of Christ and the Rapture of the church. And Revelation 12:7-8 says that, one day, Michael and his angels will be victorious over Satan and all the forces of darkness in the last conflict of the age.

Gabriel: Gabriel means "Mighty One of God." And in Luke 1:19, Gabriel describes himself as one "who stands in the presence of God." Gabriel is a special messenger angel—and he always brings good news. He answered Daniel's prayer at the end of the Babylonian captivity. Five hundred years

> *I say to you that in heaven their angels always see the face of My Father who is in heaven.*
>
> —Matthew 18:10

later he announced the birth of John the Baptist. And it was Gabriel who announced the birth of Jesus Christ.

Who in the skies above can compare with the LORD? Who is like the LORD among the heavenly beings?

—Psalm 89:6, NIV

DO ANGELS RECEIVE SALVATION?

Redemption is not a personal reality for angels, but they are excited about it on our behalf. According to 1 Peter 1:12, "Even angels long to look into these things" (NIV). The angels actually rejoice when people are saved: "I tell you, there is rejoicing in the presence of the angels of God over one sinner who repents" (Luke 15:10, NIV). But they cannot testify personally to something they have not experienced. This means that throughout eternity, Christians alone will give personal witness to the salvation that God made possible when the Lord Jesus wiped our sin away and gave us His righteousness.

If then you were raised with Christ, seek those things which are above, where Christ is, sitting at the right hand of God. Set your mind on things above, not on things on the earth. . . . When Christ who is our life appears, then you also will appear with Him in glory.
—Colossians 3:1-2, 4

Heaven's Rebels

WHAT ARE "ANGELS OF LIGHT"?

There are two kinds of angels in the world. There are the real angels of God, and then there are what the Bible calls "angels of light." Angels of light are not good. That term is a reference to the evil angels. Paul warns us that "Satan himself masquerades as an angel of light" (2 Corinthians 11:14, NIV). These angels rebelled against their created purpose; Beelzebub—the "ruler of the demons" (Matthew 12:24)—is their leader.

The ability of Satan and his ministers to transform themselves into angels of light is a very real deception, so it is of upmost importance that we recognize that not every angel is from God. That's why 1 John 4:1 instructs us to "test the spirits, whether they are of God; because many false prophets have gone out into the world."

HOW MANY ANGELS REBELLED AGAINST GOD AND FOLLOWED SATAN?

There is a strong indication that Satan was able to draw one-third of the angels into joining his rebellion. And that is what demons are: the angels who fell with Satan and came to be his servants on this earth. Revelation 12:4 says the dragon's "tail drew a third of the stars of heaven and threw them to the earth." And we know from the use of the word *stars* in the book of Revelation that stars refer to angels (Revelation 8).

> *The third angel sounded his trumpet, and a great star, blazing like a torch, fell from the sky on a third of the rivers and on the springs of water—the name of the star is Wormwood.*
>
> —Revelation 8:10-11, NIV

HOW COULD SATAN REBEL AGAINST GOD? DO ANGELS HAVE FREE WILL?

It is an interesting thing to consider: Why didn't God prevent Satan from rebelling? Didn't He know what would happen when He created Satan? Yes, God could have prevented it, because He is omnipotent. And surely He knew what would happen, because almighty God is omniscient—He knows all. The answer lies herein: Satan was created exactly as we are—with freedom to choose. God creates His creatures with full choice.

This day I call the heavens and the earth as witnesses against you that I have set before you life and death, blessings and curses. Now choose life, so that you and your children may live and that you may love the LORD your God, listen to his voice, and hold fast to him.

—Deuteronomy 30:19-20, NIV

WHERE DO DEMONS RESIDE?

The Bible speaks of two kinds of demons: the "fallen and the free" and the "fallen and the imprisoned."

The "fallen and the free" angels are the wicked spirits that work as Satan's agents here upon the earth and create havoc in our world today. But when we read the Bible in 2 Peter 2:4 and again in Jude 1:6, we learn that there's a whole group of these fallen angels who aren't free. They are the "fallen and the imprisoned"—a class of the fallen angels that we know as demons who are already imprisoned in a place called Tartarus, one of the compartments of hell, where they are reserved for judgment.

WHY ARE SOME DEMONS FREE AND SOME IMPRISONED?

Scripture says these angels "did not keep their proper domain" (Jude 1:6). And this isn't talking about their original sin when they fell with Satan. Many theologians believe that the imprisoned angels are the ones who were guilty of the unnatural sin mentioned in Genesis 6:2, when the fallen angels saw "the daughters of men" and cohabited with them, producing offspring that were half-angelic and half-human. These angels violated God-given boundaries when they left their proper domain and came into the realm of humanity to pursue a relationship that God never intended them to have.

WHAT HAPPENS TO DEMONS?
CAN THEY BE REDEEMED?

Living in the presence of almighty God, these angels rebelled against Him—and they are doomed to eternal punishment in the "everlasting fire prepared for the devil and his angels" (Matthew 25:41). The demons are without hope, for Jesus Christ did not shed His blood at Calvary to redeem the fallen angels. Christ's precious blood was shed for mankind—for the world of lost men and women.

> *God did not spare the angels who sinned, but cast them down to hell and delivered them into chains of darkness, to be reserved for judgment.*
>
> —2 Peter 2:4

When the Pharisees heard it they said, "This fellow does not cast out demons except by Beelzebub, the ruler of the demons."
But Jesus knew their thoughts, and said to them: "Every kingdom divided against itself is brought to desolation, and every city or house divided against itself will not stand. If Satan casts out Satan, he is divided against himself. How then will his kingdom stand?
—Matthew 12:24-26

Angels and You

DO I HAVE A "GUARDIAN ANGEL"?

As far as I can determine, there are just two verses in the Bible that indicate there might be guardian angels in the world today. The first is Matthew 18:10: "Take heed that you do not despise one of these little ones, for I say to you that in heaven their angels always see the face of My Father who is in heaven." Apparently, some of God's angels are assigned to stand ready before the Father to respond instantly to His command for protection and care over these children. Jesus calls these particular angels "their angels." And that's why some people have used this passage as proof that everyone has an angel.

The second passage that seems to support guardian angels is in Acts 12. After Peter was released from jail, he went to the home of Mary, where a group of Christians was praying for his release. A servant named Rhoda answered Peter's knock at the door. She was so excited to hear his voice, she left him outside and ran to tell the believers Peter was at the door. They didn't believe her and reasoned the person at the door must be Peter's angel.

Now, those are the only two passages that I'm aware of that allude to the idea of guardian angels. Having said all of that, let me also present to you the other side of the story, because while many believers throughout church history have believed in guardian angels, others have rejected the idea, feeling these two texts are not proof enough to construct such a doctrine. As you read the Scripture, there were many times when more than one angel was called into action on behalf of one of God's chosen. Several angels carried Lazarus's soul to Abraham's bosom. And Elisha and his servant were surrounded by many angels. The psalmist writes that all the angels rally for the protection of one saint.

Now, we can't know with absolute certainty whether or not each believer has a guardian angel; but we do know that God's angels care about us and that they can intervene in our lives as they are called by God—and that's a wonderful thought!

WHAT PURPOSE DO ANGELS SERVE?

Our English word *angel* translates the Hebrew word *mal'ak* in the Old Testament and the Greek word *angelos* in the New Testament. The core meaning of both of those words is "messenger." That's the essence of who and what angels are: God's messengers.

God's will and work for angels is to communicate His messages, both by what they say and what they do (Psalm 103:20-21). And solely in obedience to His will are they sent to serve us. God's own ministry to us, His plans for us, and His protection of us are the busy stairway angels use in their daily diligence of attending to our needs. When they give us strength or enlightenment, it is God's strength or enlightenment that they impart (Luke 22:43; Daniel 9:21-22). Their encouragement is God's encouragement (Genesis 16:10-11). Their guidance is God's guidance (Acts 11:13). Their protection is God's protection (Psalm 34:7). When they bring comfort and assistance, it is God's comfort and assistance they offer (Matthew 4:10-11). And when they bring wrath, it is God's wrath they inflict (2 Chronicles 32:21). Through what angels say and do, God personally expresses to us His friendship, His fatherhood, and much more.

CAN I ASK ANGELS FOR ASSISTANCE?

The Bible gives no indication that angels will respond if we pray directly to them for help. We are never told to pray to angels. In fact, in Scripture we don't find any instances of people even asking God to send them an angel's protection. And the only person in Scripture who tried persuading someone else to seek help from an angel was Satan, who quoted an Old Testament verse about angelic protection while tempting Jesus in the wilderness (Matthew 4:6).

Angels are God's messengers to us and never our messengers to God—they are not go-betweens or mediators between us and heaven. No one in Scripture ever prayed to an angel, and neither should we. We pray to God, and He sends the help we need.

WHY ARE ANGELS INVISIBLE TO US ON EARTH?

One reason that angels are invisible to humans may be that, if they were seen, they would be worshiped. Man, who is so prone to idolatry as to worship the works of his own hands, would hardly be able to resist the worship of angels were they before his eyes.

Twice in the book of Revelation, John was confronted by an angel and tried to worship him. Both times the angel told him not to worship him but to worship God.

In his book *Angels: Ringing Assurance That We Are Not Alone*, Billy Graham suggests another reason that we are unable to see angels:

> While angels may become visible by choice,
> our eyes are not constructed to see them
> ordinarily any more than we can see the
> dimensions of a nuclear field, the structure
> of atoms, or the electricity that flows through
> copper wiring. Our ability to sense reality is
> limited. . . . So why should we think it strange
> if men fail to perceive the evidences of angelic
> presence?[4]

There must be quite a lot of intervening angels around that we just never notice—but sometimes, when the time is right, God takes the scales off our eyes so we can see them. In Numbers 22:31, Balaam's eyes were opened to see the "Angel of the LORD," and in 2 Kings 6:16-17, the Lord opened the eyes of Elisha's servant to see the "horses and chariots of fire" surrounding Elisha.

I, John, am the one who heard and saw these things. And when I had heard and seen them, I fell down to worship at the feet of the angel who had been showing them to me. But he said to me, "Don't do that! I am a fellow servant with you and with your fellow prophets and with all who keep the words of this scroll. Worship God!"

—Revelation 22:8-9, NIV

DO ANGELS EVER APPEAR IN
HUMAN FORM?

Yes, some angels appear in human form. In Genesis 18 and 19, angels appear as men to Abraham and Lot. If you read the story carefully, you see that these angels ate, washed, walked, grabbed hands—they took a physical form.

Hebrews 13:2 says, "Do not forget to entertain strangers, for by so doing some have unwittingly entertained angels." If you really believe in angels and would enjoy entertaining or honoring them (as a thank-you gesture perhaps for everything they do for you), consider improving your hospitality to strangers. Not until eternity will you know if any of the strangers you encountered were angels, but the possibility is exciting!

IN HEAVEN, WILL BELIEVERS BECOME ANGELS?

According to the Bible, angels are a created class of beings and are never represented as spiritually progressed men. In other words, people do not evolve into angels. Angels do not age, nor do they spend time trying to earn

> *Do not forget to entertain strangers, for by so doing some have unwittingly entertained angels.*
>
> —Hebrews 13:2

their wings. They were all created simultaneously—in a single moment. Their full number was created in the beginning, and there has been no increase in their ranks since that time. God's angels exist eternally—as they were created.

If you say, "The LORD is my refuge,"
and you make the Most
High your dwelling,
no harm will overtake you,
no disaster will come near your tent.
For he will command his
angels concerning you
to guard you in all your ways;
they will lift you up in their hands,
so that you will not strike your
foot against a stone.
—Psalm 91:9-12, NIV

The Ultimate "Extreme Makeover"

WHEN WILL WE RECEIVE OUR NEW, GLORIFIED BODIES?

When believers die, their bodies go into the grave until the Resurrection at the Rapture. On that day, Christ is going to come in the air, the trumpet will sound, and those who have died in Christ are going to be raised up. In the process of the Resurrection, at the last trumpet, the bodies of believers will be immediately transformed into their permanent, heavenly bodies—in the twinkling of an eye (1 Corinthians 15; 1 Thessalonians 4).

On that day, Christ is going to come in the air, the trumpet will sound, and those who have died in Christ are going to be raised up.

WHAT IF OUR EARTHLY BODIES ARE DESTROYED?

In 1 Corinthians 15, Paul writes, "What you sow, you do not sow that body that shall be, but mere grain—perhaps wheat or some other grain. But God gives it a body as He pleases, and to each seed its own body" (verses 37-38).

Paul is using an illustration here. If you put a kernel of corn into the ground and let it grow, the green stalk that comes out of the ground is not the kernel. It's part of the kernel; it represents the kernel; but it's not the same as the original kernel. In other words, the body that comes out of the grave on the day of resurrection is different from the body that went into the grave.

Whether we have a body in a grave to be resurrected or our body is destroyed by fire or some other disaster, an incorruptible body will be resurrected to join with Christ in the air on that great day.

WHAT WILL OUR GLORIFIED BODIES LOOK LIKE? WILL WE JUST BE "FLOATING SPIRITS"?

While we don't know all the details about our future bodies, Scripture indicates that they will resemble the resurrected body of Jesus (Philippians 3:20-21; 1 Corinthians 15:49).

After He was resurrected, yet before His ascension, Jesus said His body was real. He even invited His disciples to touch Him—"for a spirit does not have flesh and bones as you see I have" (Luke 24:39). And when we get to heaven, we're not going to be disembodied spirits that float around forever; we're going to have real bodies—physical, transformed bodies like the body of the Lord Jesus when He was resurrected from the grave.

We're going to have real bodies—physical, transformed bodies like the body of the Lord Jesus when He was resurrected from the grave.

WILL WE BE IDENTIFIABLE IN HEAVEN? WILL OUR FRIENDS AND LOVED ONES KNOW US?

We will be recognizable in heaven, just as Christ was identifiable to His disciples when He returned to earth after His resurrection. John 21:12 describes the scene this way: "Jesus said to them, 'Come and eat breakfast.' Yet none of the disciples dared ask Him, 'Who are You?'—knowing that it was the Lord." But we will have new physical bodies that are designed for heaven, not earth.

> *When we all get to heaven,*
>
> *What a day of rejoicing that will be!*
>
> *When we all see Jesus,*
>
> *We'll sing and shout the victory!*
>
> —Eliza Hewitt and Emily Wilson

---∽∾---

Shall we know one another in Heaven?
… We are told that we shall be like our
Lord Jesus … and does He not know
and love and remember? He would
not be Himself if He did not, and we
should not be ourselves if we did not.[5]
—Amy Carmichael

---∽∾---

WILL OUR BODIES REALLY BE ETERNAL? OR WILL OUR HEAVENLY BODIES EVENTUALLY PASS AWAY?

Our present bodies are buried in corruption, but our resurrection bodies will be incorruptible. According to 1 Corinthians 15:40-42, "There are also celestial bodies and terrestrial bodies; but the glory of the celestial is one, and the glory of the terrestrial is another. There is one glory of the sun, another glory of the moon, and another glory of the stars; for one star differs from another star in glory. So also is the resurrection of the dead. The body is sown in corruption, it is raised in incorruption." That's right—our bodies will last for eternity! They will be incapable of deterioration. They will never get old or tired and will never be subject to accidents or disease or aging. We will be free from pain and decay and disabilities and death—forever.

We will be free from pain and decay and disabilities and death—forever.

WILL WE STRUGGLE WITH OUR SIN NATURE IN HEAVEN?

The Bible says that when we are transformed and our resurrection bodies come out of the grave, we are going to be totally controlled by the Spirit (1 Corinthians 15:42-53). The natural body is soul-controlled, but the spiritual body will be Spirit-controlled—completely made over, transformed, and no longer governed by the appetites of the flesh. This means we're going to do only those things that please the Lord. Our physical appetites will be marginalized by the appetite that we have for the Lord God and His glory.

The spiritual body will be Spirit-controlled—completely made over, transformed, and no longer governed by the appetites of the flesh.

Heaven's Oscars

WHAT KINDS OF REWARDS WILL BELIEVERS RECEIVE IN HEAVEN?

The Bible clearly lists at least five crowns that will be awarded in heaven.

1. The first crown is the Victor's Crown. This crown will be awarded for self-discipline (1 Corinthians 9:25-27).

2. The second is the Crown of Rejoicing, which will be given to those who have led others to Christ (1 Thessalonians 2:19).

3. The third is the Crown of Righteousness, which will be given to those who have a longing for the Lord Jesus—who look for Jesus' return (2 Timothy 4:8).

4. The fourth is the Crown of Life, placed upon those who have endured and triumphed over trial and temptation and persecution, even to the point of martyrdom (James 1:12; Revelation 2:10).

5. The fifth is the Crown of Glory, awarded to the faithful shepherds of the people of God and to Christian leaders (1 Peter 5:4).

These are not by any means the only rewards that will be distributed in heaven. But above all, it is important to remember that the

No crown could ever compare to the splendor of seeing our Lord and Savior face-to-face.

Lord Himself is our chief reward. No crown could ever compare to the splendor of seeing our Lord and Savior face-to-face.

WHEN WILL HEAVENLY REWARDS BE DISTRIBUTED? WILL THERE BE SOME KIND OF "AWARDS CEREMONY"?

The Bible tells us that one day, after all believers are removed from the earth at the Rapture, individual believers are going to stand before the Lord Jesus Christ at the judgment seat (sometimes referred to as the bema seat), where the Lord is going to judge us for our conduct and work as believers:

- "Each of us [believers] shall give account of himself to God" (Romans 14:12).
- "We must all appear before the judgment seat of Christ, that each one may receive the things done in the body, according to what he has done, whether good or bad" (2 Corinthians 5:10).
- "Each one's work will become clear; for the Day will declare it, because it will be revealed by fire; and the fire will test each one's work, of what sort it is. If anyone's work which he has built on it endures, he will receive a reward" (1 Corinthians 3:13-14).

On that day we will be given rewards for what we have done as believers between the moment of our salvation and the day that we ultimately stand before Him.

IS APPEARING BEFORE THE JUDGMENT SEAT OF CHRIST A FINAL EXAM FOR HEAVEN?

While Christ does evaluate our works, our appearance before the judgment seat is not an entrance exam for heaven. Our sins have been paid in full by Christ at Calvary, so any works of man do not qualify us for acceptance to that eternal resting place. The judgment seat of Christ is where you will be rewarded for your Christian service as a believer after you have entered into heaven.

You will be rewarded for your Christian service as a believer after you have entered into heaven.

WHAT IS THE ULTIMATE GOAL OF ANY REWARDS WE MAY RECEIVE IN HEAVEN?

With all the rewards that we will be eligible to receive in heaven, this question remains: What are we going to do with them?

After receiving our rewards, we are going to see Jesus. In response, we're going to take the crowns that He's given us, fall down at His feet, and cast them before the throne as a gift of love, saying:

> You are worthy, O Lord,
> To receive glory and honor and power;
> For You created all things,
> And by Your will they exist and were created.
> REVELATION 4:10-11

At that glorious moment, we will have the opportunity to give to Christ the only thing we have to offer Him in heaven other than ourselves. And take my word for it—we won't want to be empty-handed!

We know in part and we prophesy in part, but when completeness comes, what is in part disappears. . . . Now we see but a poor reflection as in a mirror; then we shall see face to face.
—1 Corinthians 13:9-10, 12, NIV

The Heavenly City

ARE HEAVEN AND THE NEW JERUSALEM THE SAME PLACE?

The new Jerusalem is an actual, physical city located within the third heaven. Jesus referred to the new Jerusalem as the "city of My God" in Revelation 3:12. And one day, this holy city is going to descend from heaven. We read in Revelation 21:2 that John "saw the holy city, New Jerusalem, coming down out of heaven from God, prepared as a bride adorned for her husband." Since we know that God dwells in the third heaven, we can assume that He is preparing this city in the third heaven—the city which will eventually become the "capital" of heaven and the final abode of His children. During the Millennium, the new Jerusalem will hover over the earth; during the eternal state, it will rest upon the ground. It will be the most incredible city anyone has ever beheld.

CAN ONE CITY REALLY ACCOMMODATE ALL THE BELIEVERS WHO HAVE EVER LIVED?

Heaven's capital will easily be able to house all of the people who have ever trusted in Christ since the very beginning of time. And this heavenly city will not be crowded by any means. Notice what John says in Revelation 21:16: "its length, breadth, and height are equal," each "wall" measuring twelve thousand furlongs. This means the New Jerusalem is about 1,500 miles wide, 1,500 miles long, and 1,500 miles high—that's more than 2 million square miles on the first "floor" alone! And given that this city is cubical, we can assume that it will have more than one level. Remember, we cannot fathom the grandeur of this place. It will be unlike anything we have ever seen, and there is no question that it will be able to house every believer who has ever lived.

ARE DESCRIPTIONS OF HEAVEN LIKE "PEARLY GATES" AND "STREETS OF GOLD" JUST FOLKLORE?

Gates made of pearl, foundations of precious stones, streets of gold ... we've all heard these descriptions of heaven—imagery that may at first sound like fantasy—but these heavenly features are directly from the Scriptures. In the book of Revelation, John gives us a glimpse of the new Jerusalem in all its majesty:

> She had a great and high wall with twelve gates, and twelve angels at the gates.... The construction of its wall was of jasper; and the city was pure gold, like clear glass. The foundations of the wall of the city were adorned with all kinds of precious stones: ... jasper ... sapphire ... chalcedony ... emerald ... sardonyx ... sardius ... chrysolite ... beryl ... topaz ... chrysoprase ... jacinth ... amethyst. The twelve gates were twelve pearls: each individual gate was of one pearl. And the street of the city was pure gold, like transparent glass.
>
> REVELATION 21:12, 18-21

Can you imagine approaching heaven's capital—seeing it from afar? A magnificent city built upon gemstone foundations, each gate brilliantly crafted from a single pearl, streets poured from the purest gold, a magnificent light emanating from the throne of God. This is the new Jerusalem described in Scripture. And one day, we're going to walk into this holy city with jaws dropped and eyes widened in absolute wonder, for even the most beautiful places on earth don't hold a candle to what God has envisioned for those of us that have placed our trust in Him.

WHAT ARE THE TREES OF LIFE AND THE RIVER OF LIFE?

Do you remember Psalm 46:4? "There is a river whose streams shall make glad the city of God." Well, there really is a river in the heavenly city—"a pure river of water of life, clear as crystal, proceeding from the throne of God and of the Lamb" (Revelation 22:1). On each side of this river are twelve trees of life, "each tree yielding its fruit every month." And the leaves of the trees are "for the healing of the nations." (Revelation 22:2) The word *healing* in the Greek language is the word *therapeia*—the same word from which we get our term *therapeutic*. So eating from the tree will not enhance our holiness, because we will be perfectly holy, but it will be therapeutic, giving us a greater sense of fulfillment, pleasure, and joy at being in the presence of God.

WHAT IS HEAVEN'S LIGHT SOURCE? DOES HEAVEN ORBIT THE SUN, SIMILAR TO A PLANET?

In Revelation 21 we read: "The city had no need of the sun or of the moon to shine in it, for the glory of God illuminated it. The Lamb is its light" (Revelation 21:23).

The Lord Jesus will be the light, and there will be no need for any other source.

In the new Jerusalem there will be no light posts, no lanterns, and no lamps. Light emanates from the throne of God, where the Lamb who is the Lord Jesus is seated. He will be the light, and there will be no need for any other source, because the light of the Lord Jesus in His glorification will fill the city with brilliance. What a spectacular image!

HAS ANYONE EVER BEEN GIVEN A GLIMPSE OF HEAVEN?

The Bible tells us that John was given a vision of heaven. He saw a door open and found himself peering through a portal into heaven itself (Revelation 4:1-2). When God allowed John to see a glimpse of the beauty, brilliance, and worship in heaven, John obtained a new perspective on his life here on earth. His exile in Patmos, though difficult, was seen in view of the home that God has prepared for us—a home that is just as real as our temporary dwelling but is inexplicably glorious and will last for all eternity.

God has prepared for us a home that is just as real as our temporary dwelling but is inexplicably glorious and will last for all eternity.

Worship in Heaven

IS PRAYER GOING TO BE AN INTEGRAL PART OF OUR LIVES IN HEAVEN?

The Bible says we are going to spend eternity in praise and worship. But as far as we know, there is no prayer in heaven. Why? We will be dwelling in the presence of almighty God, living in the light of His every good wish for us, and enjoying personal fellowship with our Lord. With this in mind, we can gather that there will be no need to pray.

Whether there are prophecies, they will fail; whether there are tongues, they will cease; whether there is knowledge, it will vanish away. For we know in part and we prophesy in part. But when that which is perfect has come, then that which is in part will be done away.

—1 Corinthians 13:8-10

WHAT WILL WORSHIP BE LIKE IN HEAVEN?

John was allowed to see heavenly worship. And in Revelation 4, he wrote about the magnificence of that occasion.

Verse 4: "Around the throne were twenty-four thrones, and on the thrones I saw twenty-four elders [the representatives of the church of the living God] sitting, clothed in white robes; and they had crowns of gold on their heads."

Verse 6: "Before the throne there was a sea of glass, like crystal. And in the midst of the throne, and around the throne, were four living creatures full of eyes in front and in back."

Verses 8-11: "They do not rest day or night, saying: 'Holy, holy, holy, Lord God Almighty, who was and is and is to come!' Whenever the living creatures give glory and honor and thanks to Him who sits on the throne, who lives forever and ever, the twenty-four elders fall down before Him who sits on the throne and worship Him who lives forever and ever, and cast their crowns before the throne, saying:

'You are worthy, O Lord, to receive glory and honor and power; for You created all things, and by Your will they exist and were created.'"

Oh, how I wish we could see and hear all that John describes to us in these passages. One day we will be a part of that great gathering before God's throne—bringing honor and glory to the Lord.

> *You are worthy, O Lord, to receive glory and honor and power; for You created all things, and by Your will they exist and were created.*
>
> —Revelation 4:11

WILL THERE BE CHURCHES IN HEAVEN?

John tells us in the book of Revelation: "I heard a loud voice from heaven saying, 'Behold, the tabernacle of God is with men, and He will dwell with them, and they shall be His people. God Himself will be with them and be their God'" (21:3). Speaking of the holy city, John goes on to say, "I saw no temple in it, for the Lord God Almighty and the Lamb are its temple. . . . They shall see His face, and His name shall be on their foreheads" (21:22; 22:4).

It is an interesting and strange thing to fathom, but there really won't be need for preaching or church buildings or sanctuaries in heaven. The Bible says we will know our Lord even as we are known (1 Corinthians 13:12). We will have a complete grasp of the things of God. And frankly, that's what makes heaven a reality. It's not the streets of gold or the gates of pearl or the angels. Heaven is heaven because God the Father is there and Jesus Christ is there. At last, all the barriers will be removed, and we will be able to know God in a way that we cannot possibly comprehend in this life.

Heaven is heaven because God the Father is there and Jesus Christ is there.

WHY WORSHIP NOW IF I'M GOING TO SPEND ALL OF ETERNITY WORSHIPING?

Worship is not about us; it's about God. One of the main purposes of worship is to get our minds off the things of this earth and onto the things of heaven. That's why we read in Colossians 3 that we are to set our mind "on things above, not on things on the earth," for we've died and our life is hidden with Christ in God (verses 1-3).

We were created to worship God. One day, we're going to be involved in a gigantic worship experience when we praise the Lord together in heaven.

Worship is the avenue that leads us from the emptiness of this world to the fullness of the next world. It is the street that leads from decay and discouragement to renewal and glory; and when we fail to worship, we confine ourselves to the despair of this life.

Some people are indifferent about worship, but I believe worship is the very core of our existence. We were created to worship God—and not just on our own but together with the body of Christ. And one day, we're going to be involved in a gigantic worship experience when we praise the Lord together in heaven. So let's start rehearsals, because there's no guarantee how much time we'll have to get ready—it could be tomorrow!

—— ❧ ——

"[Worship is] to quicken the conscience
by the holiness of God, to feed the mind
with the truth of God, to purge the
imagination with the beauty of God,
to open the heart to the love of God, to
devote the will to the purpose of God."
—William Temple

—— ❧ ——

What on Earth Is the Millennium?

WHEN WILL THE MILLENNIUM TAKE PLACE?

Now, it might not immediately seem important—what a person believes about the timing of the thousand years—but a person's interpretation of that thousand-year period affects his or her interpretation of other passages and events in the Bible.

Church history has seen the rise of three competing views.

Postmillennialism: This is the view that the Second Coming will follow the Millennium. As more and more people are converted, the world will gradually be conquered for Christ. At that time, God's justice will prevail across the earth, and Jesus will return to take up the throne that was won for Him by His church.

Amillennialism: This is the view that there is no literal Millennium. In other words, the events that are in Revelation 20 are happening right now, and the church is reigning with Christ over the earth. This view often stems from an allegorical interpretation of the book of Revelation.

Premillennialism: This is the oldest of the three views and is the view that I believe to be accurate. Premillennialism is based on a literal interpretation of Scripture and teaches that the Second Coming will precede the Millennium. This would place the Millennium after the Rapture and after the seven years of tribulation. Then Jesus Christ will come back and literally reign on the earth for a thousand years.

WHERE DOES THE TERM *MILLENNIUM* APPEAR IN THE BIBLE?

Before we can address this question, we must understand the term itself. *Millennium* is a Latin word which is made up of two root words: *mille*, which means "a thousand," and *annum*, which means "years." So the word *millennium* means "a thousand years."

Revelation 20 is the only place in the Bible where that actual phrase appears; and it appears in the text six different times.

Verse 2: "He laid hold of the dragon, that serpent of old, who is the Devil and Satan, and bound him for a thousand years."

Verse 3: "That he should deceive the nations no more till the thousand years were finished."

Verse 4: "They lived and reigned with Christ . . . a thousand years."

Verse 5: "The rest of the dead did not live again until the thousand years were finished."

Verse 6: "Over such the second death has no power, but they shall be priests of God and of Christ, and shall reign with Him a thousand years."

Verse 7: "When the thousand years have expired, Satan will be released from his prison."

WHAT WILL LIFE BE LIKE DURING THE MILLENNIUM?

During the Millennium there will be no war; it will be a time of previously unknown joy, purity, peace, and prosperity (Isaiah 2:2-4). Sin will be kept in check and disobedience will be dealt with. Christ's Kingdom will be a holy Kingdom. And we will spend that thousand-year period ruling and reigning over the earth with Jesus as our King (Revelation 5:9-10).

> *The Millennium will be a time of previously unknown joy, purity, peace, and prosperity.*

WHAT IS THE PURPOSE OF
THE MILLENNIUM?

There are a number of reasons that a literal Millennium must occur.

To reward the people of God: There are scores of promises scattered throughout the Bible, both in the Old Testament and in the New Testament, guaranteeing God's people that they will receive rewards for faithful service (for example, Matthew 16:27; Matthew 25:34; Revelation 22:12). And part of our heavenly reward will be to reign and rule with Christ upon this earth during the Millennium. Each of us will have opportunities to serve the Lord based upon our faithfulness in serving Him right now.

To receive an answer for the disciples' prayer (Matthew 6:8-13): One day, when Jesus returns, His Kingdom will come and His will shall be done on this earth.

To reemphasize man's depravity and the necessity of Christ's death: During the Millennium, those faithful servants who survive the Tribulation will bear children, in whom the sin nature will reside, because the fallen human nature of man will not

Man can never achieve righteousness apart from God.

be eliminated until eternity begins at the end of the millennial kingdom. At the end of the thousand years, Satan will be released, and he will stir up a final rebellion against God just as he did in the Garden of Eden (Revelation 20:1-3, 7-8). That's right—even though Christ is ruling and reigning on the earth during the Millennium, some will yet be deceived. This demonstrates just how deeply man needs a Savior. Man can never achieve righteousness apart from God.

WHAT HAPPENS WHEN THE MILLENNIAL PERIOD COMES TO A CLOSE?

At the end of the thousand years, two things will happen:

Revelation 20:7-10 tells us that after Satan has been loosed for a short season of rebellion, he will be cast into the lake of fire and brimstone, where he will reside for eternity.

The Great White Throne Judgment will also take place at the close of the Millennium. But believers will not be present at this judgment, because the purpose of this judgment is not to determine who is lost or saved. Rather, all who have rejected Christ throughout history will be judged according to their works. And on that day, those whose names do not appear in the Book of Life will be cast into the lake of fire (Revelation 20:11-15).

All who have rejected Christ throughout history will be judged according to their works.

The New Heaven
and the New Earth

WHEN WILL THE NEW HEAVEN AND NEW EARTH BE CREATED?

The new heaven and the new earth will not appear until the Rapture, the Tribulation, the Battle of Armageddon, the Millennium, and the Great White Throne Judgment have all taken place. Once these events have happened, almighty God is going to create the new heaven and new earth. Here is John's description of his vision: "I saw a new heaven and a new earth, for the first heaven and the first earth had passed away. Also there was no more sea. Then I, John, saw the holy city, New Jerusalem, coming down out of heaven from God, prepared as a bride adorned for her husband. And I heard a loud voice from heaven saying, 'Behold, the tabernacle of God is with men, and He will dwell with them, and they shall be His people'" (Revelation 21:1-3).

Almighty God is going to create the new heaven and new earth.

IS THE NEW EARTH THE SAME EARTH WE LIVE ON TODAY?

In 2 Peter 3 we are told that "the heavens will pass away with a great noise, and the elements will melt with fervent heat; both the earth and the works that are in it will be burned up" (verse 10). However, the phrase "burned up" doesn't appear that way in the early Greek manuscripts. The original word in the text conveys the idea of being uncovered or laid open for exposure. In other words, Peter is not talking about destroying the earth; he is telling us that at the end of the Millennium, as God is preparing for the eternal state, He is going to do a refreshing of the earth. God is going to destroy all the evidences of decay, disobedience, and disease. But He's not going to annihilate the world in which you and I currently live; He's going to purify it from all of the old corruption. He's going to create a new heaven and new earth.

The very things which make this life difficult—sorrow, pain, death—should serve as reminders that we, as believers, are not home yet.

The very things that make this life difficult—sorrow, pain, death—should serve as reminders that we, as believers, are not home yet. Christ is preparing a home where His people will dwell with Him forever (John 14:2-3).

Behold, the tabernacle of God is with men,
and He will dwell with them, and they
shall be His people. God Himself will be
with them and be their God. And God
will wipe away every tear from their eyes.
—Revelation 21:34

WILL THERE BE SEAS IN THE NEW HEAVEN AND EARTH?

Currently three-fourths of the earth is covered in salt water; but the apostle John tells us that in the new earth, there will be "no more sea" (Revelation 21:1).

The ecology of the new heaven and earth will be entirely different than that of the earth we live on today. And there will be no need of salt water, because salt is a preservative, and there will be no decay. But there will be fresh water in the new heaven—the river of life, flowing from the throne of God in the new Jerusalem, which will rest upon the ground during the eternal state. These waters will be more beautiful than any landscape we can fathom in this life.

WILL SIN'S CURSE BE GONE ONCE AND FOR ALL?

Because of Adam's sin, there was a curse on all creation: "Cursed is the ground for your sake; in toil you shall eat of it all the days of your life. Both thorns and thistles it shall bring forth for you, and you shall eat the herb of the field. In the sweat of your face you shall eat bread till you return to the ground, for out of it you were taken; for dust you are, and to dust you shall return" (Genesis 3:17-19). But in the new earth, there will be no more curse—and no more sin! For the thousands and thousands of millennia that roll on in the eternal state, Revelation 22:3 says "there shall be no more curse, but the throne of God and of the Lamb shall be in it, and His servants shall serve Him."

In the new earth, there will be no more curse—and no more sin.

Tough-Minded
about Heaven

HOW SHOULD I LIVE TODAY IN LIGHT OF ETERNITY?

What we think about heaven determines how we live today. We can easily be led away from God's purposes if we do not steadfastly pursue the things of God and His will (2 Peter 3:17); and without diligence, we can be lulled into apathy and ungodliness, which bring no joy to God or to our personal lives. C. S. Lewis once said, "If you read history you will find that the Christians who did most for the present world were just those who thought most of the next."[6]

How do we become effective for Christ in our present world? We must make sure that our lives are matching the purpose for which we were created. We must be diligent to pursue God's righteousness through the Word, prayer, purity, and seeking His will. That's the way to live in light of eternity—in light of the "glorious appearing of our great God and Savior" (Titus 2:13).

We must make sure that our lives are matching the purpose for which we were created.

The grace of God that brings salvation
has appeared to all men, teaching us that,
denying ungodliness and worldly lusts,
we should live soberly, righteously, and
godly in the present age, looking for the
blessed hope and glorious appearing of
our great God and Savior Jesus Christ.
—Titus 2:11-13

*Scripture
Reference Guide*

HEAVEN SCRIPTURE REFERENCE GUIDE

Psalm 46:4: There is a river whose streams shall make glad the city of God, the holy place of the tabernacle of the Most High.

Matthew 16:27: The Son of Man will come in the glory of His Father with His angels, and then He will reward each according to his works.

Matthew 18:3-4: Assuredly, I say to you, unless you are converted and become as little children, you will by no means enter the kingdom of heaven. Therefore whoever humbles himself as this little child is the greatest in the kingdom of heaven.

Matthew 25:21: His lord said to him, "Well done, good and faithful servant; you were faithful over a few things, I will make you ruler over many things. Enter into the joy of your lord."

Matthew 25:34: The King will say to those on His right hand, "Come, you blessed of My Father, inherit the kingdom prepared for you from the foundation of the world."

John 14:2-3: In My Father's house are many mansions; if it were not so, I would have told you. I go to prepare a place for you. And if I go and prepare a place for you, I will come again and receive you to Myself; that where I am, there you may be also.

Romans 14:12: Each of us shall give account of himself to God.

1 Corinthians 3:13-14: Each one's work will become clear; for the Day will declare it, because it will be revealed by fire; and the fire will test each one's work, of what sort it is. If anyone's work which he has built on it endures, he will receive a reward.

1 Corinthians 15:51-52: We shall not all sleep, but we shall all be changed—in a moment, in the twinkling of an eye, at the last trumpet. For the trumpet will sound, and the dead will be raised incorruptible, and we shall be changed.

2 Corinthians 5:10: We must all appear before the judgment seat of Christ, that each one may receive the things done in the body, according to what he has done, whether good or bad.

Ephesians 4:10: He who descended is also the One who ascended far above all the heavens, that He might fill all things.

Philippians 3:20-21: Our citizenship is in heaven, from which we also eagerly wait for the Savior, the Lord Jesus Christ, who will transform our lowly body that it may be conformed to His glorious body.

Colossians 3:1: If then you were raised with Christ, seek those things which are above, where Christ is, sitting at the right hand of God.

1 Thessalonians 4:14-16: If we believe that Jesus died and rose again, even so God will bring with Him those who sleep in Jesus. . . . We who are alive and remain until the coming of the Lord will by no means precede those who are asleep. For the Lord Himself will descend from heaven with a shout, with the voice of an archangel, and with the trumpet of God. And the dead in Christ will rise first.

2 Timothy 4:8: Finally, there is laid up for me the crown of righteousness, which the Lord, the righteous Judge, will give to me on that Day, and not to me only but also to all who have loved His appearing.

Hebrews 9:27-28: As it is appointed for men to die once, but after this the judgment, so Christ was offered once to bear the sins of many. To those who eagerly wait for Him He will appear a second time, apart from sin, for salvation.

James 1:12: Blessed is the man who endures temptation; for when he has been approved, he will receive the crown of life which the Lord has promised to those who love Him.

1 Peter 5:4: When the Chief Shepherd appears, you will receive the crown of glory that does not fade away.

2 Peter 3:10: The day of the Lord will come as a thief in the night, in which the heavens will pass away with a great noise, and the elements will melt with fervent heat; both the earth and the works that are in it will be burned up.

Revelation 2:10: Be faithful until death, and I will give you the crown of life.

Revelation 4:9-11: Whenever the living creatures give glory and honor and thanks to Him who sits on the throne, who lives forever and ever, the twenty-four elders fall down before Him ... and cast their crowns before the throne, saying: "You are worthy, O Lord, to receive glory and honor and power; for You created all things, and by Your will they exist and were created."

Revelation 20:6: Blessed and holy is he who has part in the first resurrection. Over such the second death has no power, but they shall be priests of God and of Christ, and shall reign with Him a thousand years.

Revelation 20:11-12: Then I saw a great white throne and Him who sat on it, from whose face the earth and the heaven fled away. And there was found no place for them. And I saw the dead, small and great, standing before God, and books were opened. And another book was opened, which is the Book of Life. And the dead were judged according to their works, by the things which were written in the books.

Revelation 20:15: Anyone not found written in the Book of Life was cast into the lake of fire.

Revelation 21:1: Now I saw a new heaven and a new earth, for the first heaven and the first earth had passed away. Also there was no more sea.

Revelation 21:2-3: Then I, John, saw the holy city, New Jerusalem, coming down out of heaven from God, prepared as a bride adorned for her husband. And I heard a loud voice from heaven saying, "Behold, the tabernacle of God is with men, and He will dwell with them, and they shall be His people. God Himself will be with them and be their God."

Revelation 21:4: God will wipe away every tear from their eyes; there shall be no more death, nor sorrow, nor crying. There shall be no more pain, for the former things have passed away.

Revelation 21:16: The city is laid out as a square; its length is as great as its breadth. And he measured the city with the reed: twelve thousand furlongs. Its length, breadth, and height are equal.

Revelation 21:22-23: I saw no temple in it, for the Lord God Almighty and the Lamb are its temple. The city had no need of the sun or of the moon to shine in it, for the glory of God illuminated it. The Lamb is its light.

Revelation 21:27: There shall by no means enter it anything that defiles, or causes an abomination or a lie, but only those who are written in the Lamb's Book of Life.

Behold, I am coming quickly, and My reward is with Me, to give to every one according to his work.

—Revelation 22:12

Revelation 22:1-2: He showed me a pure river of water of life, clear as crystal, proceeding from the throne of God and of the Lamb. In the middle of its street, and on either side of the river, was the tree of life, which bore twelve fruits, each tree yielding its fruit every month. The leaves of the tree were for the healing of the nations.

Revelation 22:3-4: There shall be no more curse, but the throne of God and of the Lamb shall be in it, and His servants shall serve Him. They shall see His face, and His name shall be on their foreheads.

Revelation 22:12: Behold, I am coming quickly, and My reward is with Me, to give to every one according to his work.

ANGELS SCRIPTURE REFERENCE GUIDE

1 Kings 22:19: I saw the Lord sitting on His throne, and all the host of heaven standing by, on His right hand and on His left.

Psalm 91:11, NIV: He will command his angels concerning you to guard you in all your ways.

Psalm 103:20-21: Bless the Lord, you His angels, who excel in strength, who do His word, heeding the voice of His word. Bless the Lord, all you His hosts, you ministers of His, who do His pleasure.

Daniel 10:5-6: I lifted my eyes and looked, and behold, a certain man clothed in linen, whose waist was girded with gold of Uphaz! His body was like beryl, his face like the appearance of lightning, his eyes like torches of fire, his arms and feet like burnished bronze in color, and the sound of his words like the voice of a multitude.

Matthew 18:10: Take heed that you do not despise one of these little ones, for I say to you that in heaven their angels always see the face of My Father who is in heaven.

Matthew 22:30: In the resurrection they neither marry nor are given in marriage, but are like angels of God in heaven.

Luke 15:10: There is joy in the presence of the angels of God over one sinner who repents.

Luke 16:22: So it was that the beggar died, and was carried by the angels to Abraham's bosom. The rich man also died and was buried.

Luke 20:35-36: Those who are counted worthy to attain that age, and the resurrection from the dead, neither marry nor are given in marriage; nor can they die anymore, for they are equal to the angels and are sons of God, being sons of the resurrection.

John 1:51: He said to him, "Most assuredly, I say to you, hereafter you shall see heaven open, and the angels of God ascending and descending upon the Son of Man."

Hebrews 1:7: Of the angels He says: "Who makes His angels spirits and His ministers a flame of fire."

Hebrews 1:13-14: To which of the angels has He ever said: "Sit at My right hand, till I make Your enemies Your footstool"? Are they not all ministering spirits sent forth to minister for those who will inherit salvation?

Hebrews 12:22-23: You have come to Mount Zion and to the city of the living God, the heavenly Jerusalem, to an innumerable company of angels, to the general assembly and church of the firstborn who are registered in heaven, to God the Judge of all, to the spirits of just men made perfect.

Hebrews 13:2: Do not forget to entertain strangers, for by so doing some have unwittingly entertained angels.

Revelation 5:11: Then I looked, and I heard the voice of many angels around the throne, the living creatures, and the elders; and the number of them was ten thousand times ten thousand, and thousands of thousands.

Revelation 10:1: I saw still another mighty angel coming down from heaven, clothed with a cloud. And a rainbow was on his head, his face was like the sun, and his feet like pillars of fire.

Do not forget to entertain strangers, for by so doing some have unwittingly entertained angels.

—Hebrews 13:2

Revelation 19:11, 14: Now I saw heaven opened, and behold, a white horse. And He who sat on him was called Faithful and True, and in righteousness He judges and makes war. . . . And the armies in heaven, clothed in fine linen, white and clean, followed Him on white horses.

Additional Resources by
Dr. Jeremiah

Agents of the Apocalypse

Are we living in the end times? What if the players depicted in the book of Revelation were out in force today? And if they were, would you know how to recognize them? In this book, Dr. Jeremiah explores the book of Revelation through the lens of its major players: the Exile, the martyrs, the 144,000, the two witnesses, the dragon, the beast from the earth, the beast from the sea, the Victor, the King, and the Judge. Each chapter opens with a dramatization that brings prophecies to life, followed by a detailed study that explores some of Revelation's most cryptic passages, explaining how to interpret them and—most important—how they apply to the malevolent forces at play in the world today.

Angels: Who They Are and How They Help

People have long been fascinated by angels, yet many contemporary beliefs about angels are based on misconception and myth rather than solid, biblical truth. In *Angels*, Dr. Jeremiah provides answers to many questions people have about these celestial beings. Through careful study of the Scriptures, he separates fact from fiction to discover who angels are—and how they help!

31 Days to Happiness: Searching for Heaven on Earth

In this book, Dr. Jeremiah examines the writings of history's most successful man, Solomon, in the book of Ecclesiastes. Through this careful study we learn that Solomon was a man who tested life's haunting questions head-on—and tasted life's riches full-on—and found his answers in the last place he thought to look. If you have been searching for happiness, perhaps you, too, have been looking in all the wrong places. Learn more in *31 Days to Happiness—Searching for Heaven on Earth*.

My Heart's Desire

Has your worship lost its wonder? In this stirring study on worship, Dr. Jeremiah invites you to rediscover worship and explore what it means to encounter God every moment of every day. Revive the wonder in your walk with God and satisfy your heart's desire as you experience the presence of God through a passionate lifestyle of praise and reverence.

Captured by Grace

Grace is just a word until it happens to you. Encountering God's grace changes lives forever. Let Dr. Jeremiah show you how the transforming mercy that captured songwriter John Newton and the apostle Paul can awaken within you a fresh experience of the God who loves you unconditionally and pursues you with abandon. Have you been captured by grace?

What Are You Afraid Of?

For many people, worry, anxiety, and fear are constant companions: fear of death, fear of danger, fear of disease. And too often these fears are crippling, keeping us from the life God has called us to live. But it doesn't have to be that way, says Dr. David Jeremiah. As Christians, we have been given all we need in order to face down even the most frightening, unexpected, and overwhelming obstacles in life. In *What Are You Afraid Of?* Dr. Jeremiah explores the top nine fears that are holding so many of us back from the life God has called us to live and shares the supernatural secrets for facing down these fears with faith.

Notes

1. Doris Kearns Goodwin, *No Ordinary Time* (New York: Simon & Schuster, 1994), 464.
2. William R. Newell, *The Book of the Revelation*, 9th ed. (Chicago: Moody Press, 1935), 334.
3. Randy Alcorn, *Heaven* (Carol Stream, IL: Tyndale House Publishers, 2004), 414.
4. Billy Graham, *Angels: Ringing Assurance That We Are Not Alone* (Nashville: Thomas Nelson, 1995), 23–24.
5. Amy Carmichael, "Thou Givest . . . They Gather," quoted in *Images of Heaven: Reflections on Glory*, comp. Calvin Miller, Lil Copan, and Anna Trimiew (Wheaton, IL: Harold Shaw, 1996), 111.
6. C. S. Lewis, *Mere Christianity* (New York: Macmillan, 1960), 134.

About the Author

Dr. David Jeremiah serves as senior pastor of Shadow Mountain Community Church in El Cajon, California. He is the founder and host of Turning Point, a ministry committed to providing Christians with sound Bible teaching relevant to today's changing times through radio and television, the Internet, live events, and resource materials and books. A bestselling author, Dr. Jeremiah has written more than forty books, including *Captured by Grace, Living with Confidence in a Chaotic World, What in the World Is Going On?, The Coming Economic Armageddon, God Loves You: He Always Has—He Always Will,* and *What Are You Afraid Of?*.

Dr. Jeremiah's commitment to teaching the complete Word of God continues to make him a sought-after speaker and writer. His passion for reaching the lost and encouraging believers in their faith is demonstrated through his faithful communication of biblical truths.

A dedicated family man, Dr. Jeremiah and his wife, Donna, have four grown children and eleven grandchildren.

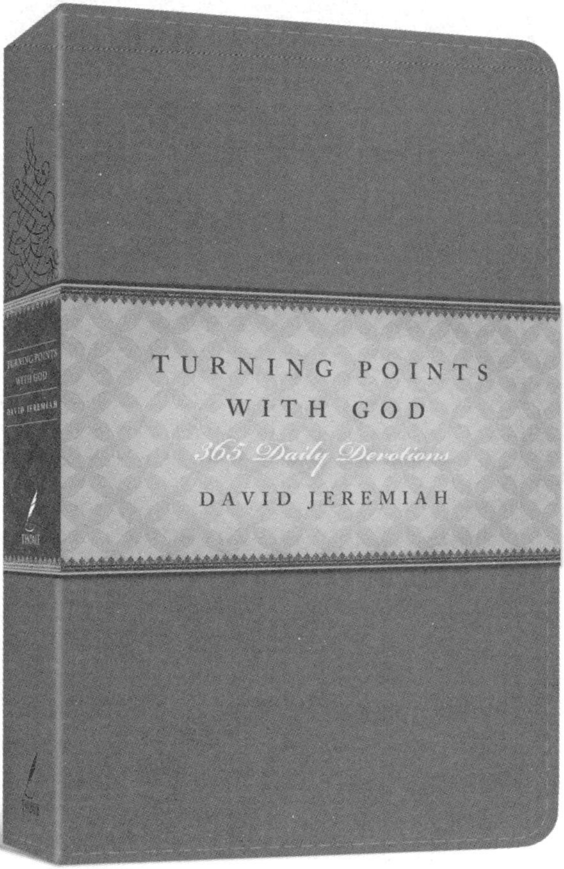
TURNING POINTS
WITH GOD
365 Daily Devotions
DAVID JEREMIAH